*Learning Shouldn't Stop*
*When You Do*
By
Cherie S. Garland, M.Ed., Ed. S.

Copyright © 2016 Cherie S. Garland, M.Ed., Ed. S.
Published in the United States by Cherie S. Garland
CreateSpace is the Printing Platform
World-wide distribution by amazon.com

All rights reserved.

ISBN-13: 978-1535563291
ISBN-10: 153556329X
.

*Sinking of A Sub: Learning Shouldn't Stop When You Do* is printed as a First Edition and made possible by a one-time gift-in-kind offer from Wayne Drumheller, M.Ed., Editor and Founder, The Creative Short Book Writers' Project for book design, editing assistance and writing encouragement. The quotes and notes found in this book are, to the best of her ability, what the author heard, felt, believed and remembered when they were spoken, read or inferred to her. No part of this book may be reproduced or transmitted in any form or by any means, electronic or mechanical, including photocopying, recording or by any information storage and retrieval system without permission from the editor, except for brief quotations embodied in articles or otherwise specified

# DEDICATION

*Sinking of a Sub* is dedicated to the men and women who brave the unexpected and turbulent job of taking care of students in the absence of the teacher. They are to be commended for their dedication and tenacity. Without the substitute teacher, learning would not go on when we are out. Thank you!

# ACKNOWLEDGEMENT

I would like to acknowledge all of my cool colleagues and administrators at O.T. Bonner Middle and G.W High. I also acknowledge LaSheera Lee who is always pushing me and making me accountable for my success. Thank you Hubby, Mommy, Bishop Alicia Patterson, Sir Anthony Patterson and Pastors Pete Hairston and Annie Hairston. Your prayers are acknowledged and they have not been in vain. A special thanks to my beautiful editor and daughter, Nikki. Finally, I'd like to acknowledge and thank the thousands of children who education has afforded me the privilege of teaching and loving. You are the wind in my back.

# Introduction

Let's face it, I signed up because I lost my job at Walmart, my car payment was due, and I knew that the school system was desperate for warm bodies.

I didn't even know I was highly qualified for the gig until Franklyn Jones, the Fifth Street bum, said one afternoon when I was out on the street looking for coins, "Girl, you can sign up to be a substitute teacher!"

Normally, I would have ignored "Frankie the Freeloader," but the idea that such an elite position was something I was qualified for made me stop dead in my tracks and listen.

I asked, "What you say man?" Frankie, grinned with all three teeth and said it again, but this time he attached some evidence to the statement.

"Yeah, you know my girlfriend don't even have a legal address, and she's a sub." So, now I'm really interested because the last time I stepped foot in a school was the high school graduation, and that was to see my twin sister cross the line. I was on a ten-day suspension, and I was trespassing even then! Oh, did I introduce myself? My name is Ms. Tonie, and I'm a substitute.

We've all thought it, but never said it. Substitutes are just that--sub teachers. We take the place of--fill in, replacements, and the list goes on and on. If you are wondering about the qualifications for being a sub, (and I'm talking about the *real* qualifications, not the fake ones that they have posted on the school division's website) here they are.

- **Qualification One:** You need a high school diploma or a GED. *(This is what I have).* Some divisions require an Associate's or even a Bachelor's degree.

- **Qualification Two:** You have to be able to pass a basic skills test *(Which I did).*

- **Qualification Three:** You must have the strength and elasticity of a conveyor belt. Did I mention you have to be able to contort your **pedagogical** mind in all different directions?

*I read about that word in a book on a third grade teacher's desk. By the way, that is* **Qualification Four.**

And finally,

- **Qualification Five**: You have to be able to swim because when the ship, or in my case, the submarine is going down, you don't want to drown!

I know what you're thinking. If you are a teacher you're shaking your head from side to side and making clicking noises with your teeth. You know something like, "Tsk tsk tsk." However, if you are a sub, you're thinking, "Girl, I know just what you mean!" Your water logged, bloated body tells it all.

I know teachers, you don't have a clue,

because if you did, you would have shut this book a

long time ago, hung your head in shame, found a

sub, any sub, and given her your last paycheck *and*

some flowers.

The truth is that the danger is not in your

student's lack of respect for who we are, it is not

because we are unqualified (Which most are*).* If we

**were** qualified, we'd be called professional part-

time, intermediate, or qualified replacement--but we

are called substitutes!

And, like it or not, that's what we are! A

subpar facsimile of the real deal! The impending

danger results from a lack of or faulty planning,

which makes it hard for a substitute to deliver proper

instruction that supports learning when you are

5

absent. Look at the statistics. Teacher shortage areas are increasing; therefore substitutes are becoming a vital part of the educational arena.

Oh, back to the impending danger. Chances are, we subs never took a computer course, chances are we think an Elmo is the red, furry puppet on Sesame Street™, and chances are we never used a copy machine except for the one at Kmart. *Truth be told, I jammed that one trying to make a copy of my Social Security Card.*

So how do you sink a sub? *Oh NO, this is not a "How to Sink a Sub" guide! Although subpar, we know how valuable we are. Without us, you would be applying for the job I got fired from at Walmart.* We are the ones that make it possible for you to take a break, to get away from the mayhem. We allow you to take that "sick" day every now and then.

Like it or not, it is important that you take really good care of us so we'll be around for the next job, and the next one, and the next. That's right. Subbing **is** a full time job, and although we are not the real thing, we **must** be able to stay afloat in your classroom. Your success depends on it.

I present to you seven vital lessons to consider when planning your absence. Although you can't

possibly make the subbing experience a perfect one, you can surely put these seven lessons into practice so that your sub can walk away from the job knowing that your children's learning didn't stop because you did.

# SINKING OF A SUB!

The call came in at 6:04 a.m. There was something about that ring that let you know it was **not** an emergency call from a sick child or an ailing parent. It rang with a different kind of urgency-- almost threatening. You answer the phone knowing that you wouldn't hear a warm human voice on the other end. The voice would be monotone and unfeeling. You listened and found out that it is for Mrs. Muncie's fifth grade class; the one where the little boy cursed you and told you that he didn't have to listen to a dumb sub, 'cause his Aunt TuTu was a sub and she didn't even have a car and you probably don't have one either... *Uh little boy, **THAT** would be Frankie the Freeloader's girl!* You could've hung up that phone, stayed in bed, and watched reruns of Scandalous all day, but duty called and so

did your car payment. *Yes little boy, I do have a car*

*payment and that's why I'm subbing in the first*

*place otherwise I'd be relaxing on the sandy beach.*

So you press "one" to accept the job. You listened

for further instructions because hopefully they will

help you figure out the mess that you will have to

swim through when you arrive at Mrs. Muncie's

room. Now what's wrong with Muncie's plans?

SINKING OF A SUB

# Lesson Number One:

## TEACHERS, NEVER LEAVE A LESSON THAT YOU HAVE NOT TAUGHT!

We are the replacements, remember? We aren't authentic. We did not graduate from Harvard, take a Praxis, complete five months of student teaching, and most of us are not equipped to introduce a lesson. How-be-it, Mrs. Muncie leaves an introductory lesson on adding fractions. *I felt the water swirling around the bottom of my feet.*

Let's see, the lesson plan said, "Have the students turn to page thirty-three, read over the directions with them, complete number one on the board, and then let them do two through two

hundred. Reteach for those who do not understand."

*The water was rising.*

Teach? Reteach? Mrs. Muncie, you don't really

want **me** to teach fractions! I really did want to

follow her instructions; however, that same little boy

was sitting right there ready to sink this sub. He had

that look on his face. You know the one that said he

was about to talk about Aunt TuTu, FuFu, ChuChu;

or whatever her name was. He was watching me

and waiting for me to make a mistake. And believe

it or not, I was intimidated!

Could you please, Mrs. Muncie and all her

fellow sub sinkers leave practice sheets that reflect

what the children have already learned?  Please?  I am well equipped to help them, but starting from scratch is a sure set up for sinking.

Well the little boy saw me struggling and gave me the "My Aunt is a sub and she doesn't have a car" line. *The water was around my ankles now, which was all the motivation I needed to call my bestie, Carol, and ask her to explain how to add one fourth and two eighths.  There was no shame in my game, because I had a car payment to make at the end of the month. Carol was the "Fraction Beast," so I figured this might enable me to hold back the rising waters.*

Mrs. Muncie had, for the final activity, a movie about a wildlife reserve that the children would view.  Did she have a VCR?  NO!  Did she

have a DVD player? NO!  Did she even have a TV?

OF COURSE NOT!  Mrs. Muncie expected **me** to

find the YouTube Channel on her computer, turn on

the projector, and show the movie on the white

board screen.  Really?  I didn't even know how to

find YouTube!

I heard your thoughts, you sub sinkers.  "Ask

the kids, call the teacher next door, or ask for the IT

personnel."

Sinkers, think about it!  By the time I'd gone

through all of those changes, that little boy and his

partners in crime would've been hanging from the

ceiling tiles!  After all, they'd already started making

paper ships out of the math work we didn't

complete, and I'm not 100% sure if what I…

I mean Carol "taught" was even correct. *The day ended with me knee deep in water, but much to that little boy's chagrin, I didn't drown!*

# Lesson Number Two:

## PLEASE DON'T MAKE THE SUB DEPEND ON TECHNOLOGY TO EXECUTE YOUR PLANS!

Technology is as effective as the sub using it. The nightmares that flood my mind are continuously on instant replay. Like a relay race, one thought is ending as the other passes the baton and hands it off to the next one.

Mr. Dick! Oh the memories. If you are chuckling at this point, imagine what it was like on that wonderful January 2nd. The day after returning from a three week, Christmas, lying around the house doing nothing but playing with your

PlayStation 6- break. *Oh, that's not out yet? I'm sorry! I lost count…* Well, PlayStation 4, or whatever!

Just imagine, these kids had been relaxing for days without interruption, except to take another sour candy worm out of the bag and munch it into oblivion! Mr. "D," as I prefer to call him, was on an extended vacation because he "had the flu." *Pause. That's why you need this book, sinkers. You know you're going to take that "flu break" every now and then!* Where was I? Oh yeah, Mr. "D" the Robotics teacher at Tech Charter High.

His plans read, "Students will work on their robotics design. Refer to the manual on the desk for troubleshooting."

That was it? In other words, these ninth graders were going to run the class. I was a glorified, paid babysitter. That sounded good to me!

First of all, the students obviously loved this class because they came flooding in like it was the state fair, and they were giving away free rides. One-by-one, then two-by-two they filed in until every seat was filled. They looked, and noticed that Mr. "D" was not in place. *I felt the water rising around my feet.*

Student one, with a grimace on his face, said, "Hey Miss, you know anything about Robotics?"

Student two, shot a glance at a suspecting friend, "Hey ma'am, you friends with (pause) MR. DICK?"

*The water was definitely around my knees now.*

A stream of chuckles filled the lab. I stood, moved throughout the room and glanced at every student, I mean I periscopically looked them dead in the eye, no, in BOTH EYES! Even the little prima donna who looked like she wouldn't hurt a goldfish; I aimed at her too.

I started, "Listen to me, every one of you!"

*Did I hear waves? The water was at my waist!*

*Yeah, I was sinking!*

I went on, "I am not your everyday ordinary sub, I have been given instructions on how to conduct this class, and Mr. "D" as **you** will refer to him, has given me permission to troubleshoot anyone who gives me a problem! YOU HEAR?"

Silence, glances, squinty eyed stares, puffy cheeks

holding in air with hand over mouths, and then the

release--the class erupted in laughter. I stomped

over to the desk, opened the troubleshooting manual,

and there, in front of me, were diagrams, arrows,

codes and all kinds of computer terms that I am sure

were written in Japanese because it didn't look like

English to me! *The sub was definitely sunk!*

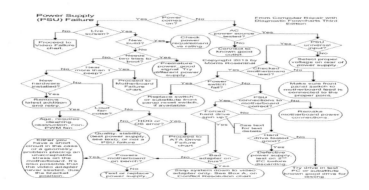

The class was now so out of control that I sat

and watched the rowdy crew throw paper balls, and

airplanes. Although my underwater vision was cloudy, I realized that I did learn the definition of trouble-shooting, which, although I doubt it would prevent another catastrophe, taught me a relevant term. That, sinkers, is the irony of the job. Subs actually do wind up becoming rather "school literate." And some of us, if pulled ashore and resuscitated, actually do become professional subs.

If you are a sub and you are reading this book, I know you be insulted by my reference to the lack of qualifications. Of course, this is a generalization, because I have met subs who kept the class in better control than the teacher. I know you. I've seen the teachers roll their eyes at you as you sauntered down the hallway with your tidy little class of cadets, ready to tackle the day's events like a well-trained

commander. You are the envy of the school and

definitely among the ranks of degreed, or school

diplomats; however, none-the-less, suffering subs.

For the sake of the message, it is imperative that we

let our sinkers feel the plight of the less than

qualified majority. Remember, some of us don't

have a car, and at least one of us doesn't even have a

legal address.

# Lesson Number Three:

## PLEASE BE CAREFUL WHO YOU ASSIGN AS YOUR "GO TO KID!"

Mr. Danzie's classroom is a SPED, self-contained and multi-aged group. I know that it is hard for a teacher to find a "go to kid" in a small setting; however, a sub would rather not have one than to endure the struggle of depending on children who are not dependable. The first time I subbed for Danzie I thought it would be the last!

The cool thing about subbing is you feel a slight sense of power because you can say "NO" anytime you want to!

*Now, let's get back to the teacher. He's the kind of guy that you call "Danzie." I don't know if it's the ponytail or the bell bottoms, but there's just something about him that makes you feel weird calling him Mr., and I am not the only one who feels that way! Even the principal, who calls everyone Mr. or Ms. calls Danzie, "Danzie."*

Oh, let me get back to "The Go To Kid." Danzie left really explicit plans for the nine different subjects and levels for the nine students in his classroom. It was like unbaking baked spaghetti, but, for the most part, I conquered

that. There was no new lesson to teach, no

technology, just really great planning.

The problem was his "go to kids."

Danzie wrote in bold letters, **"If you need**

**anyone to run an errand, ask Joey or Angelica**."

Normally, there is something so comforting about

being on a boat with your "go to" kid, and this time

there were two! I felt confident, victorious, and

equipped for smooth sailing. However, problem one

occurred when I couldn't figure out whether all of

the children attended specials at the same time. (The

only thing that was unclear in Danzie's plans).

Today's special was P.E., so, I asked Joey to go to

the gym to ask Mrs. Myers, the P.E. teacher, which

children should report to the gym.

He confidently rose from his seat and said, "Yes Ma'am."

I noticed a surprised look on a few of the children's faces. *Is that water I hear?* Well, as it turned out, Joey left at 10:15, and at 10:22, he had not returned. *The waves are dashing against my knee caps. This sinking is going down!*

Worried, I asked Angelica to go find Joey.

Everyone, even Angelica, looked puzzled. *I feel the water at my belly button.* Angelica squirmed in her seat.

The other children raised their hands. "Yes?" I responded questioningly. In unison, the seven children said, "Angelica's the new girl. She doesn't know her way around."

*I felt a wet tickle on my chin.*

27

Then, one of the seven shouted, "Joey runs

away sometimes. He mighta did it again!"

*I gasped for air, my arms flailed, I tried to stay*

*afloat, but it was too late! I sunk!*

Reporting the remainder of the day is futile.

The long talk with Joey's mother about how I need to

consider another "career!" The whispers at

lunchtime, the Amber Alert--let's not even discuss

the police report! All of this because Danzie chose

two "go to kids" who were clueless. Sinkers, try

your "go to kids" out. Put them through a trial run.

Let them practice, but please don't sink the sub by

leaving your weakest allies in charge.

# Lesson Number Four:

## PLEASE LEAVE DETAILED EMERGENCY PLANS!

Sinkers...please, please, pretty please leave specific, detailed, legible, and easily accessible emergency protocols.  The date was October 6, and I was called to BonAire Middle School,  an elite institution on the Southeast side of town.  You know, where all of the doctors and lawyers live.  It's school that sits on the 9th hole of the exclusive golf course.  The school that is rumored to only hire teachers with Master's degrees or higher to work there--and rumor has it that unless there is a mass epidemic like the flu, only two professional subs, last names Weinerth and Jacobson, (coincidentally, the names of two local doctors) sub at the school. Rumor also has it that the school has provided their professional subs with a small lounge, equipped with a coffee maker, *Mademoiselle* Magazines, TV with cable, **and** a microwave. Rumor also has it that Weinerth and Jacobson's kids attend the school, so when they drop them off, they conveniently stay and work when needed. *I bet those two never sink.*

If a plain old sub like me gets a call from BonAire, there is an epidemic or a staff development that requires at least three subs.

Well, October 6, I was that third sub.

The absentee was a 24-year-old, Harvard grad, Ms. Pasteur. When I got the call, I initially wanted to decline it because it was a very cold morning, and due to the previous three days of rain, it was a damp one too. However, I took the job when I heard it was BonAire. I got a big kick out of sitting in **their** private little lounge and reading *Mademoiselle* while sipping on **their** coffee. I could always feel the hate, as they side eyed me during breaks.

That particular day, I arrived ahead of time and was pleased to enter a sterile and brightly colored room. Ahhhh, fourth grade, I thought! I surveyed the room. Her plans were immaculate! Her desk was organized, and everything was labeled and color-coded. There was absolutely no room for error. The nerves I had expended on preparing

31

myself for the bourgeoisie experience left me with only a few to operate on. I mustered up the nerves I had left and actually had a very successful morning.

There is something sweet about fourth graders. They still believe lies and they have some type of reverence for subs. The lies that didn't work with my middle and high schoolers worked with these BonAire fourth graders. Lies like, "If you don't do what you need, I am going to video call your teacher and let her see what is going on in this room!" "Yes ma'am," they would say as they scrambled back to their seats.

Lunch was at 11:00 a.m. and it was time to change to third block when suddenly the tornado horn blew. I immediately grabbed the classroom attendance roll, (I knew to do at least that much), and without my telling them to, those fourth grade sailors lined up and proceeded to the hallway. I saw a child go down on his knees and face the wall.

"Boy if you don't get up off your knees!" I shouted. "Pray later!" I continued. The hustle and bustle of the hallway came to a dead standstill.

"LET'S GO!" I said in my loudest voice. "GO OUTSIDE and don't make a sound!"

"But Miss..." a small, adorable little boy started.

"THIS IS NOT THE TIME FOR A BUT!" I shouted.

"If one of you so much as opens your mouth you are going to get a Facetime™ visit from Ms. Pasteur." Silence, stifled cries, tears, sniffing.

"OUTSIDE OR FACETIME™!" I shouted even louder.

The thought entered my mind. *Why was it taking so long for the others to come outside? And for God's SAKE, why was every one of these fourth graders crying and pointing?*

Folks, there are times when silence is NOT golden. The fourth graders used my obvious confusion as an opportunity to break the muddy silence.

A little prissy thing squeaked, "Ms. Lady, this is a tornado drill, and we are supposed to be on the floor **inside** with our faces pointing to the wall and our arms over our head and we **gotta be** on our

34

knees." *I faintly heard the sounds of waves*

*crashing.* I wanted to rebut, but the fact that we'd

been out there alone for about two minutes unnerved

me. I'd asked for someone to raise their hand and

tell me what wall we should be facing when I saw

Weinerth and Pasteur, the elite subs, standing in the

hallway shaking their heads. Pasteur is using her

cell phone to call someone and give them a firsthand

report.

"You're supposed to be inside!" yelled

Weinerth.

By then, the children were hysterical, and

crying their eyes out. The water, now around my

neck was approaching my nose when I realize, I'm

sunk, hook, line and sinker! So sinkers, please leave

detailed plans regarding any and all emergencies.

Little ones will freak out, middle schoolers will manipulate the drill, and high schoolers will swim to the nearest hangout when the sub doesn't know how to handle a drill, or, God forbid, a true emergency.

# Lesson Number Five:

## PLEASE MAKE YOUR OWN COPIES!

This is one of the greatest lessons of all time.

Not just for sinkers, but for subs too. I learned so

much about teachers in the copy room.  If you want

to discover the true nature of teachers, just hang

around that huge, loud, paper spitting, often broken

down robotic monster called, "The Copying

Machine."  If you want to make a teacher mad, just

stand there and try to make four hundred copies for Miss Gregory's history class at Loyalton Middle, while a last minute copier is waiting for you to finish.

The call was a weird one, and I should have known better than to take it; however, inexperience in educational matters will sometimes leave you treading some awfully dangerous waters. When the phone rang, it was much later than the usual electronic call. School, for everyone, had either started or was about to start. I slowly picked up the phone. It was the SECRETARY calling me. A live, not necessarily warm, but human voice spoke.

The conversation went something like this: "Ms. Toney, uh...I... uh...need a sub this morning.*giggle, giggle.*

Pause…

Silence…

"Uh...do you think you can

come...uh...be...uh...here...uh...in....like...thirty...uh

minutes?"

A longer pause and then, "Miss Gregory was

on her way to school and she um, started--you know-

-having-- uh a diarrhea--uh attack.--and uh--she had

to--go home and change.

I thought, "Lady that is too much

information!" But to save her from further

embarrassment, I cut in.

"I'll be there. Just give me time to jump in the

shower and get dressed. I'll do my best."

I learned, a long time ago, to stop making

exact time statements because if you said you would

be there in thirty minutes and you got there in thirty-

one, those secretaries treated you like **you** were the

delinquent when it was actually the teacher or the

school that caused the call to come at the last

minute! Anyway, I made it in twenty-nine minutes

because Loyalton is actually a couple of blocks from

my neighborhood.; which, is not the greatest

because, obviously, if I'm struggling to make my

car payment, I'm not living like those folks at

BonAire.

Loyalton is a job that most subs won't take.

There is almost no chance of ever walking out of

there dry. If you don't sink, you will fight three wars

to stay afloat. So you get the picture right? Oh yeah! Lest I should forget, the teachers at Loyalton have just as much attitude as the kids, if not more. It is the reason this experience is forever imprinted in my mind.

When I arrived, I noticed the plans were not well written or typed, but were scribbled down by Miss Gregory's male teaching partner, Mr. James. He wrote like a sleep-deprived physician and second-of all, there were no copies of the worksheets that she instructed me to hand out to her four classes. The students' busses were arriving, but there remained about ten minutes before anyone would actually walk through the classroom door. I grabbed a worksheet from a miscellaneous pile and made a mad dash to the copy room in the library. The librarian looked at me with pity on her face as I whizzed by. I had finally mastered copying papers after about a year of breaking down every school's machine.

*I even secretly learned how to fix a few because, although there was always a sign that said, "Please see the secretary if the machine malfunctions." First, no secretary ever stopped what she was doing to help a sub. Second, they have enough work to do; and most of the time their office is nowhere near the copy room.* Today, however, the machine seemed to be in working order.

There was one person approaching the copy room at the same time I was, so I sped up and actually beat her to the punch. She looked at me as if I had poop on my face and asked, "Who are you?" I was familiar with that question, but it was the way she said it...Yuck! *I smelled the scent of sea water in the air.* I didn't know if she was mad at me, or if she hated Miss Gregory and was taking it out on me. I laid the worksheet on the glass screen. This copier seemed so much more advanced than the usual. I started punching buttons and nothing happened. *I felt the water around my ankles.* In ran a short fair skinned lady, who apparently was trying to run off copies before the bell rang ( in two minutes and nineteen seconds).

　　She looked me up and down, although she couldn't really see above my chest.

I was still punching buttons when she asked, "What are you doing?" *My knees were wet and I hadn't even gotten to the classroom.* As she grimaced at my chest, I explained that I couldn't make the robot go into copy mode.

She stood on her tiptoes to look at the screen and asked, "What's the teacher's code?"

"Code!" I said in an alarmed tone.

She excused herself, walked right past me, punched numbers and made her copies.

"I'm sorry!" She said unapologetically. "They should have given you a code girl!"

*The sinking was inevitable.* I sheepishly tiptoed out of the room and gingerly approached the librarian.

"Ma'am?" I asked. "Could I get you to make some copies for me? I'll send a child down to get them."

She grimaced and said in the calmest voice that she could muster, because in her eyes I know I saw a blazing fire as she said,

"Sweetheart, I am the librarian, and my job is books. Honey, if I made copies all day, I wouldn't have time for books, now would I?"

*I started sinking.*

She continued, "So, you need to... (The bell rang)... go get one of those lazy secretaries to help you." And then, she concluded; "Now young lady, you have a nice day."

Did she low-key curse me out?

45

No matter what, it was clear that I didn't have time to make copies. By the time I swam to the room, children were everywhere doing everything. They asked a million questions that I didn't have any answers to, so inevitably, I spent the whole day subbing under water!

Darn that copier!

# Lesson Number Six:

## LET YOUR SUB KNOW AHEAD OF TIME If THEY WILL BE ATTENDING A FIELD TRIP!

Have you ever heard it said that when your feet hurt, everything hurts? Well, my whole body pains when I recall this subbing experience. There was nothing particularly special or different about the job. It was a typical elementary school sub call.

The name of the school escapes me. Maybe the memory is just too painful. Anyway, I accepted because it was a Friday. It my last chance to make $55.00 before payroll went in. I felt so good that I decided to dress up that day-- not a usual elementary school practice. I had one business pant-suit and a pair of three-inch stilettos for interviews. I thought it seemed like a great choice.

Most teachers would be dressed in tees and jeans on Friday, and I wanted to earn those "Who do you think you are" looks like those subs get at BonAire.

When I arrived I was directed to go to the gymnasium. This was strange because the sub call said I would be in a kindergarten classroom.

As I approached the gym, I heard chipper little voices and not so chipper big voices yelling at the little voices telling them to sit down.

I got closer and heard a little voice scream with excitement, "Mrs. Tanner, are the busses here yet?"

I waded to the gym door, slowly pulled it open, and to my surprise, there were at least 100 kindergarteners squirming in their seats.

"Oh, you must be Miss B's replacement. Thank you for coming," said a chubby veteran. The "Thank you for coming" was long and drawn out as she started peering at my shoes and scaled my entire body from head to toe, especially the toe.

"Are you sure you are going to be comfortable?

Didn't they tell you that we are going on a field trip to the zoo?" she asked, almost apologetically.

 **SINK**

*My heart sunk into the point of my stiletto, and the waves were now pushing my body to and fro.* I held on to the little strength that I had. Thinking that I had enough time to spend the $55.00 that I was about to make (bye-bye car payment) on a pair of crocs, because there was no way that I was going to walk around the zoo in three inch stilettos, I looked at my watch. There was a department store directly across the street, but just as I opened my mouth to tell the obviously concerned chubby veteran that I was going to make a mad dash to the store, I heard

the sound of diesel engines. I looked up and six

yellow submarines pulled up to escort me to my

death. *I was now choking and spitting out water.*

The walk to the busses, with my group of 25

screaming five year-olds, was a long, green mile. I

boarded the bus, *as my feet forecasted the future,*

*and sat down as the water rose above my head.* The

words "field trip" in the instructions would have

been a lifeboat for me on this last day before payroll

went in. If only I could've talked to Miss B and

given her a piece of my wet mind! I would've taken

off my three-inch stiletto and stuck it where the sun

didn't shine.

    The ride to the zoo was as expected, but there

51

was nothing more mood killing than the anticipation of excruciating pain. It almost nullified the experience. Therefore, I tried to keep my mind off of what was about to transpire in the next hour or so. Even bus monitoring was a challenge in stilettos. **YOU** try stopping two five-year-olds from pushing each other on a moving bus while wearing stilettos. If this had been a high school group, I would have been beaten up and sued after all the toes my "stingers" attacked. One little kid sort of alluded to the fact that his mother was a lawyer.

"Miss, if you stick those things in my foot one more time, my mother is going to leave her court job and come beat you up," He said, with the utmost confidence.

We arrived at the zoo as planned, and the

teacher asked me to stand outside and monitor the

children as we unloaded the bus.  Any other day this

would have been an easy task; however, in stilettos,

they might as well have asked me to carry all of the

elephants back to the school.

*Even though I was drowning, the water*

*swishing around my feet actually felt good.*

-------------------------------------------------

The final lesson is one that I learned at

Northern Middle School.  Saving the most

important lesson for last ensures committal to

memory, because this is a very crucial piece of

knowledge that will surely affect your ability to take

your "extended breaks" and "mental health days."

# Lesson Number Seven:

## PROTECT YOUR SUB FROM DISEASE!

I received the call at around ten a.m. It was for a half-day job, and I was so bored that I thought, "Hey, what can it hurt?" I even took time to stop by the deli-sub shop to get me a Turkey and Swiss. *Another sinker…not eating lunch due to lack of funds.* The instructions said that I would be taking the children to lunch---I thought it smart to pinch off some of my car payment money and indulge myself.

I arrived at Northern Middle at 10:45. *I didn't want any surprises, like a field trip, or lesson plans asking me to teach students how to build an airplane, or a directive to make 1,000 copies.* The phone instructions had also informed me that the teacher was waiting for the sub to arrive.

That was a first...*What did she do? Decide to take a half day vacation?* I stopped by the office and was directed to a second floor classroom, Number 204.

*I will never forget that! NEVER!*

When I walked in, the class was working like naval strategists. I glanced around the room. *Eighth grade," I thought, "This should be a piece of cake.*

I heard a sound, much like a stifled cough-sneeze. *You know that sound when it seems like your body doesn't know if it wants to cough or sneeze.* I looked at the teacher for the first time, and although she was a cocoa brown complexion, her nose and eyes were beet red! WHOA! She made her way towards me, and I didn't realize it, but I started backing up. I stopped and waited for her to meet me halfway.

She extended her hand...*the same one that she just removed from covering the cough-sneeze.* I wanted to place my deli-sub sandwich under my shirt to give it double protection, but I thought it best not to.

"Hi I'm--Mrs.\*\*cough\*\*cough\*\*sneeze\*\*

"Mrs. Hayes" --*with her hand still extended.* So, to

avoid making hand-to-hand contact, I fake-coughed

into my right hand hoping she would not want to

shake it. I shuddered as we made contact. "Thank

you for coming," she half smiled through her

apparent misery. I thought, "Have I even spoken

yet?" I gathered myself. "Oh…hi, I'm Ms. Tonie,"

I said with hesitance. I heard chuckles and threw a

quick glance. I was not in the mood! Not with this

lady coughing and sneezing all over the place. The

students all read me and immediately got quiet.

Then, I noticed a few of the children had their

shirt collars stretched over their noses and were

taking in oxygen in short spurts. I went to her desk,

which was covered with a mixture of balled up

Kleenex and worksheets for each of the remaining periods.

"I got these ready for you to give out to each group," she said between cough-sneezes. She took out her pen and started writing class period numbers on the top of each pile of papers. After laying the pen down, which I watched very carefully and thought, "No passes will be written today!"

She directed me to her seat.

*Lady...Mrs. Hayes...you have to be kidding me. I will be taking a seat in the very BACK of the room, and I will be letting one of your children pass out those papers, and I will be trying my best not to breathe at ALL while I'm in this room! This is a straight harpoon sinking! No gradual rise of waters*

*here! Oh no! I'm about to go down! It's a done*

*deal!*

She continued to talk about her expectations

for her students as I tried not to breathe. I think the

kids could tell, because a few pointed at me. I

steadily backed away, as she gave one more loud

cough-sneeze, and I felt it!

Sprinkles of a substance that either came from

her mouth or nose danced around on my forearm. I

spotted the hand sanitizer.

I thought, "When this lady leaves, I am going

to take a bath in that stuff!" She continued checking

and touching everything as she made her exit.

YIKES!

I assured her that everything would be okay, although I knew that it wouldn't, because she cough-sneezed all the way out of the room. Trying to remain calm and not let on that I was making a mad dash to the hand sanitizer; I introduced myself to the students while I snuck up on the life-saving liquid. I slowly picked up the bottle, looked at it as if I was reading the label, and squirted two heaping tablespoons into my right hand. Trust me; I wanted to empty the whole bottle! I gradually and inconspicuously slid the goop up and down my forearm where the cough-sneeze substance had landed.

*I heard chuckling again.*

Someone from the back, where I planned to sit, yelled, "Hey SUB! It's too late! YOU'RE SUNK!" I knew it anyway because I had already gotten the chills and the cough-sneezing had begun.

*Bubbles, blurred vision, waves...I WAS DONE!*

*Sandwich and all! Walmart, can I please have one more chance?*

So sinkers, if you are really sick this time, get someone else to run your copies, sanitize, and baptize your surfaces. When the sub arrives, please, please, please, don't expect handshakes and group hugs! After all, who will sub for the sub that's sunk?

# ABOUT THE AUTHOR

Cherie Stewart Garland, ED. S. is a 23 year teaching veteran and newly appointed high school administrator. She has served as both a substitute and a permanent teacher in Southside, Virginia and Guilford County North Carolina.

An avid play-wright and director, she enjoys teaching aspiring performers. Raised in New York by Freddie Sr. (deceased) and Margie Stewart, she developed an early love for reading and performing. Cherie is the wife of Patrick and mother/nurturer to nine beautiful human beings: E.J., Shawnta, Reggie, Nikki (Lance), Latrice, Kei.-J, P.J. (Kimberly), Ulrick and Kyla. She is grandmother to Keilijah, Kh'mari, Lucy, Israel and new additions Cameron and Anabel. Cherie is the sister to Freddie Jr (Colleen), Ronald (Mizy), Jeffrey and Chrystalyn (deceased).

She enjoys writing stories, books and plays that impact the way people treat each other. Her works share a recurring theme of compassion, honesty and transparency. As a minister of the Gospel, Cherie attributes her talents, gifts and successes to Jesus Christ.

Manufactured by Amazon.ca
Acheson, AB

11813257R00039